Loving Narcissus
&
Sometimes God

BOOKS BY TRICIA BARKER

Angels in the OR: What Dying Taught Me about Healing, Survival, and Transformation (Published by Post Hill Press, 2019)

Grateful acknowledgment is made to the editors of the following publications in which these works or earlier versions of them previously appeared:

The Binnacle (2008): "After the Wreck"

Iodine Poetry Journal (2009): "Loving Narcissus"

The Midwest Quarterly (2009): "The Magic of Crows"

Patterson Review (2008): "Cockroach beside my Toothbrush"

Ugly Accent (2007): "Persephone's Darner" and "Fool's Crush"

Best Poem (2007): "Beginning to End"

Other poems have appeared in *Ibbetson Street Press* and *The San Antonio Express News*.

First Edition, 2020

Published by Tricia Teaches, LLC

Cover art by Silvia Isachsen

Library of Congress Cataloging-in-Publication Data

Names: Barker, Tricia, Author.

Title: Loving Narcissus & Sometimes God: Poems by Tricia Barker

Description: First Edition | Fort Worth: Tricia Teaches, LLC, 2020|

Identifiers ISBN (print): 978-1-7343792-3-5

ISBN (e-book): 978-1-7343792-1-1

Subjects: Poetry, Spirituality

Tricia Teaches, LLC

www.triciabarkernde.com

Printed in the United States of America

Contents

Part 1: Loving Narcissus

Part 2: And Sometimes God

Loving Narcissus

Persephone's Darner

Persephone is gone in the winter,
and Demeter blames herself,
refusing to eat.
The effort of movement
from the bathroom to the bedroom
is strenuous,
and all the Kamut flour
has gone to hell in her cabinets.

To love someone beyond control is torture.

Memories of her small, delicate
daughter replay in her mind
and in the ether.

Persephone's light body bends and jumps
in a luminous meadow.
She is surrounded by friendly dragonflies
(Zigzag Darners, Spine-crowned Clubtails
Fine-lined Emeralds, Faded Pennants).

This child could be any child
with a step light and happy enough
to enter the world of wings.

When Hades stopped his truck beside her,
forcing her in and ending her childhood,
surely at least one Phantom Darner steeled his airy body
with dragon-like determination,
staying beside Persephone
as a witness,
strong enough to migrate
down to the underworld.

Cockroach beside my Toothbrush

There is meekness in the bow of your head
beneath your curved back,
but even humility and sensitivity
cannot save you now.
Do you remember when you
raised your folded wings at right angles
from your abdomen, showing off
the white edgings of your thorax and wing pads?
You trembled for the mate you wanted,
and she looked back at you
as if the moon glowed from inside you.
You believed passion could last forever,
denying that all we have are flashes.

Still, you never imagined this ending—
an abandoned condo by a pond,
shadows extending like frail, human arms,
no food or even cereal crumbs in the kitchen,
and only my mint-flavored, disappointing toothbrush
hanging precariously near the edge of the sink.

How could you know that surveys
list you as the most despised creature on earth?
How could you possibly deduce
that the angry fall of a boot

he left behind would become
your last moment on earth?

Thunder Bay

Moonlight scattered across the dark blue waves,
swelling, turning turquoise, breaking,
becoming foam the color of a seagull's underbelly.
A woman, wearing a silver shift,
sat meditating on a small cliff above us.
When she opened her eyes, she saw my lover
bend and spring across a ledge, agile as a deer.
Her smile widened with appreciation
and she winked at me as she shook out
her long, Venusian curls.
I looked at my lover through another's perspective,
noticing his balance and grace, the shiny lines
of energy flying out of the ends of his hair
and fingertips. I watched him and watched
the waves, knowing I would need to remember
a moment from the good year of love.

Rainy Day

I do not yearn for churches and steeples.
My love might seep out of the cracks in the wood,
and fly like tortured angels,
their tunics caught in the trees that children climb.

I cannot remember tradition, only broken pieces
and individual plans, but I can imagine
the warmth of your gaze and the softness of your neck.
I could dance in the drama of your mind
in Zimbabwe, Calcutta, or Tibet.

If I spent my life in Turkey, weaving practical rugs
to sell in town for cash, I would still breathe these similar dreams
into the patterns because inside each thought,
and each touch, a universe sways with falling stars
and rivers cutting through valleys.

A heart like mine is lacerated with shadows
of branches clawing at my window during lightning storms.
I was never afraid to run into the floods and try any path,
praying to the spirits of chance and coincidence,
anointing my forehead with the four winds
that scatter through forests and time.

How can I make you see why I must travel
great distances, chasing God inside me,
finding searing life in sunrises at the ocean,
in the sun-rayed flames around the monk Jizo,
who postponed nirvana to wander through nature
and towns with a sympathetic, approachable air?

In the clear eyes of children, calling out my name,
I have discovered the clover sweet light of Spring.
In trying to love, meaning becomes brighter than even this.

It would take eternity to name what I have found
in country fields raging with sunflowers and horseflies,
cows dipping their wide noses into warm ponds,
clanging metal barns announcing their loneliness,
but know that I am near you in dreams,
breathing a soft love that changes our world.

The Fool's Crush

In 9th grade I lost myself in tender feelings,
slow breezes, and a new heat that tumbled
down the length of my arms and legs.
School days swayed in the energy and knowing smile of Coach.
He sparkled when he walked, and I thought about his ass,
tight in the baseball uniform, and the two pictures of his wife,
plain and overweight, not a woman I imagined him with.
So, I continued to sway my newly formed hips
past his classroom and to my locker,
day after school day envisioning his suntanned hands
on my taut abdomen, the small of my back, and curve of my neck.
I continued to believe that if I visualized these moments with enough intensity,
never opening my mouth to speak, never holding his glance
for over a second, if I went home, praying on the bus
like a bright wildflower, touching myself late and night
and speaking his first name slowly, softly,
that this desire might carry across any distance—
from my pale bedroom without a door
through the pine forest behind my house,
past dairy cattle, along the black-top roads,
and into his box of a living room, reaching
like a silver hand through his TV
and gripping him.

Born into the South

abandoned
and left to play
among weeds and thorns

watched the men
gather under a sliver moon
while bob cats yelped

inside the depths
of piney woods
never believed the lies

that swarmed like gnats
around my fresh eyes and mouth
lies that justified cruel dominion

however
disbelief did not save me
from learning to hate myself

years later there were
too many ways to forget
until redemption came

only my redemption
did not resemble their kind
never based on the bible belt kind

only on amazing grace
sparrows landing near my table
soft arms of a lover

deep sleep and forgiveness
from the other side
no explanations

and no particular country
for the soul

I Refuse to Live Where Love Stops

Not here.
Not this weekend
of stale, swampy beaches,
crushed, soft-shell crabs,
and angry silence.

I am too thirsty
to drown like this.
You ask me to imagine
your pain, your sorrow,
but the wind blows
through both of us.

We have not won anything,
and I hate this highway howl,
sickle-shaped moon,
mad, polytonality of trees.
It is pointless to collect
bird bones, study voodoo
or burn amber incense.
You will continue to do
the outrageous things you do.

Love claimed me
with your ticket,
just had to have me,
but I do not like this stop,
this piece of peppermint gum,
and these hot, swaying palm trees.

I would rather be waiting
back at the track
because somebody,
at least one crazy gambler
in the bleachers,
will bet on me,
and the wind will
carry me anywhere but here.

Loving Narcissus

When Narcissus left for work,
I would put on the sandals he wore
to feel closer to him. My feet
would soak up the remnants of the love
he had for his feet, his body,
and after a while, I realized
that in his mind
I was less important
than the ground he walked on.

Narcissus on Trial

Since both the innocent and the guilty
proclaim their innocence,
Narcissus took the act farther
and decided to believe in his innocence.
He imagined he could get away with murder,
simply by shifting the focus
to what hurt him, no matter how slight the injury.

As God looks at the heart, Narcissus also gazed
into his own heart and identified beauty and confusion.
The critical difference between Narcissus and God
is that God examines everyone else's heart as well.

Narcissus and Denial

Narcissus does not know
why events turn out the way they do.
When the credits role, he sees his name
as the director of a life
astoundingly different from the one he lives.

I've watched him drink himself dizzy
and repeat a few stories he likes to tell,
caring mostly about momentary impressions—
the ones with his impression in your eyeball,
not lasting ones.

What he perceives as reality
is truth in his mind, and all things contrary
must be twisted to fit.

Narcissus is Always Right Even When Wrong

Anger is the only option
for someone who can never be wrong.
Even if the rulebook is opened
and Narcissus is shown his error,
he will defend himself.

To hate him is to compliment him
with attention. If you want justice,

give him the same indifference
he possesses for the feelings of others.
Bury him in a quiet, unmarked grave
with a single white flower
for the many women he pretended to love.

Narcissus Alone

I stood outside of him and cried,
as if he represented the concrete slabs
of a great, unfinished piece of architecture.
Cold, aborted dreams.

As an apparition, a changing memory,
a sorceress with powers he hadn't accurately measured,
I am more real to him now.
At night, I say a few words,
and he finally hears me
because I'm etched into his mind.

The Ex of Narcissus

I am still the wife of Narcissus,
waiting for divorce and wondering
why we wed. We barely made marriage
last a single season. Now, the landscape
is winter, five of swords, grass like golden hay,
and the sun wakes up close the earth.

During the day, my car makes a white streak
up and down the interstate and around the loop.
At night, I blend in with the brake lights
lost in a jumpy, erratic stream of red.

If he ever asks about me,
tell him the wind has created a minor ripple
in his vision. Give him a camera, a mirror,
a voice recorder--anything that creates an echo or image--
and he will lose reality in the reflective river of himself.

Narcissus Forgiven

Pardon him for his crimes
for he cannot see what he does to you.
Let go of how he betrayed you.
We all have a kernel
of his self-absorption.

Read your resume.
Listen to your bio.
How much of the ugly truth,
the failures, betrayals, and breakdowns
do you leave out?

You don't have to befriend Narcissus,
but forgive him
like your life depends on forgiveness.

If it is easier to cast him out,
then do it with authority in the name of Jesus.
Cast him out like a demon who pierced your heart
with ridged horns and shook the ground of your stability.

The Magic of Crows

As the city lights begin to salt the hilltops,
a woman becomes restless; her head is full of the wit
of crows, and her fate is tangled in the act of finding
one of their feathers by her doorstep. The feather feels light
in her hands, and she wonders which direction it might blow.
From her kitchen window, she observes how the crows
look like pieces of a ragged night scattered
across the final moments of the day.
They are the antithesis of stars, with a mystical sheen
of their own and wholly delighted to be crows as they
squawk into each other's faces, slowly lift one foot into the air,
or dunk their ruffled heads into the dog's bucket of water.
The woman wonders why her soup does not taste better,
why her skin does not greedily soak up the air around her,
and why these final days of summer do not burst
with the bruised pleasure of black lights, drumbeats,
and a new lover, smelling slightly of tobacco and amber,
a lover who might dip a small, velvety sumi brush
in honey, paint it on her body and then gently lick
it off while black wings flutter in the corner of her eye,
the shimmering, happy bodies of crows.

Family Dinners

The people who should
love you sometimes do not like you
as much as strangers enjoy you
and compliment your warm personality.
Sometimes these extended family members
can barely contain their simmering hate
as they pass the steaming gravy
and stay stony silent
when hearing of your good fortune.
However, these strange undercurrents and rivalries
flow from events that happened
decades before your birth.
The only thing you have done wrong
is choosing to be born
with a bright, independent spirit,
and no matter how badly they
wanted to beat it out of you
and call God the devil,
you continued to enjoy your life,
extravagantly, all the more,
despite what they thought
and said about you.

The Star Card

There are men who send their wishes on a breeze,
lost in celluloid impressions. Their yearnings circle the globe
but never pierce my atmosphere.

My years are wild light years away from most people.
They couldn't reach me with 215 million years of trying
on roads paved of gold, cocaine, and rocket fuel.

It is simply in my nature to glisten and inspire
ideas and anticipation. To them, I'm an aim,
an aspiration, an archetype, a card in a tarot deck.

Only you could read the heavens around me.
You understood my noir filters and doorways to the divine.

Once we had telepathy with our high tea and low tides.
We once had hearts that were real.

Occasionally, I allow myself to feel safe
as an ordinary woman, in plain clothes,
all the pain nicely shored-up,
until the right words penetrate me
and tears jump out of my eyes,
against my will.

There is no one I miss more than God.

Despair

Start here: You are alive,
and even the gods have made
horrible mistakes.

You have, most likely, not
used a sword to kill your only son
or worn a blindfold your entire adult life
in the name of love,
so forgive yourself
for what you have done.

Tell your heart to calm itself.
Remember a tall, protective pine tree
you knew and loved as a child.
Remember the silence you walked in
before entering this loud,
incessant den of fear.

Though you are hungry,
and your hands shake,
know that you will find
your way home,
even in the dark.

In Defense of Isolation

A room can develop a thick density that becomes hard to escape.
The air feels like something between water, shadow, and cloth,
somewhere between floating and suffocation.

Once I am certain the bolts are tightly shut,
the alarms set, and all my escape plans
and fighting plans outlined
in my over-sensitized brain,
once I know every cell of my body
is wired for 911 calls, I let go
and feel the vibration—
the beginning of something new.

Somewhere in the past, though,
it is always raining. There is always blood
and a neon light blinking on and off in a puddle.

His head makes a thud as the police officer
knocks it against the door.
I don't want to think about patterns.
I want to break them.

I want to sit here, do nothing, and release the past.
I never wanted those angry men anyway.
I picked them to save me from the crazy men.

I don't know why I mostly wanted a safe room,
but in a safe room, I wanted an impenetrable castle.
In a castle, I wanted business class trips around the world.
This is what it is like to be a woman who wants freedom
more than she wants anything or anyone.

The only true freedom I have known
is leaving my body in the place it fell,
like a discarded garment.

Blood from a Stone

No compromise from the hard ones.
No understanding in the land of mind-fuckery.
No reciprocity from darkness.
No empathy from the self-absorbed.
No integrity from the outer-focused.
No honesty from the agenda driven.
No making a point with anyone
with a false sense of superiority.

No boundaries from the narcissists.
Just the same old song and dance
of being called crazy, insecure,
and too sensitive for having a problem
with increasing levels of pain.

If you say you feel cold and alone
in the dark room where they left you,
you will be criticized for feeling cold and lonely.

A fragile ego system cannot exist in the reality
of other people's experiences.
A narcissist would rather pull the trigger
and kill love and compassion
in the eyes of the one
who is awake and real than to change.

This type of relationship played over and over again
can make a generally good person pick up a stone
and aim it hard, hoping for blood.

Dreams

Although I have a love affair with sleep,
 yearn for it during the afternoon,
fantasize about curling up in bed and surrendering to it,
I prefer its moments of oblivion
to dreams which take over my body like possessions.

My eyelids twitch and my muscles tighten and jerk
as alternate realities fume through me,
knowing the boundary of skin means nothing.
My defenseless unconscious reels through wars,
gets blown-up on-board ships, dies in a dusty land
as buildings crumble after a bomb's explosion.

I have met charlatans, patrons, and thieves.
Once, I met a magician who transformed me into a tiger,
and forced me to curl up next to the bones of Jim Morrison.
 I have been betrayed at least sixty different ways,
often by the same person. My teeth have splintered
into my gums as I tried to speak something simple,
something to save my life and the lives of others.

I've become suicidal, homicidal, and gone viral.

I've composed operas and made love to several people in one night.

Several years ago, a brown bat chased me into a dungeon

of a castle in Norfolk. Later, I begged myself blind in Mumbai,

only to feel my feet begin to burn in Salem.

Often, I wake up tired after the night's activities

and long for blissful emptiness. However, the next night,

a rattlesnake, rabid dog, or a black widow spider finds me,

and I spend what seems like hours

trying to rid myself of the poison.

Still, every night, I return to bed, without insomnia,

content to take my punishment with the relief.

Each catastrophe disappears into the smoke

of my mind, and I remember to forgive,

getting lighter with every death,

wounding, or suppressed memory.

Every nightmare brings me closer

to letting go of suffering,

closer to tranquil dreams of flying

and seeing the world turn golden.

Beginning to End

Love is a shelf of books that I have read before.
Bliss. Talking until 4 a.m.
Telling the stories of our lives.
One bookend is made of this perfection,
and the books in between are varied.
Throw in a few titles categorized
under comedy, self-help, psychology,
but mostly stick with fiction and drama.

Watch as one of the lovers
does not call or pick up the phone directly.
Feel their separation anxiety.
Strong emotions. Listen to their pleas and pledges.
Put your arms around their arms
and wish that they could stay entwined
in long, sweaty embraces.

Realize their addiction to each other,
excluding all others. Ride their tide
of their fear, irrational anger, reconciliation,
celebration, intimacy,
and then go back to fear.

Insert your own details and revisions,
but know that these two lovers
want to be together for the rest of their lives.
Observe how they desperately hang on
to their romance as their insides
tear their outsides apart.

Watch their flights and returns,
like birds going away to gather twigs.
Pity her as she falls to the floor,
and his red car speeds away
like a huge arrow shot through her.
Wounded. Betrayal. Threats.

She said the wrong thing.
He became too angry.
Fill in whatever you want to fill in.
Returned train tickets.
Even his trip to jail.
Premonitions. Angel's voices.

Just before the final bookend,
see them stranded in disbelief,
once they realize that the past
always stays in the past.
They can visit
but always alone.

Closures remind us of how quickly
our lives play out,
and how the end is always
solid and reliable.

Victim's Payback

Every time you are wounded by circumstance,
I smile.

When your car breaks down or your house needs repair,
I buy something extravagant.

When your stomach cannot digest your food,
I order more.

When you cannot get rock hard anymore,
I feel like making love.

When you die and grow cold in your grave,
I will hold on.

When people begin to forget you,
I will never remind them.

The Gaslight Club

I wish I could be air and disappear.
I wish I could be the light from the moon
in your window that you photograph,
not a woman in the next room,
waiting for connection.

I wished I needed nothing.
No eye contact. No words.
If I could love your twisted logic
(which makes me feel bad
for being me at all)
I could survive.

I wish I could be less than I am.
Anorexic. Shy.
Not here. Disappear.
I wish you could see this as a song,
as my truth,
but it will only anger you.
You'll say that I do
nothing correctly.

If I post this nowhere,
you'll accuse me of sharing it.
If I post it everywhere,
you'll ignore it or threaten me.

Wish I didn't want to the thrill of your touch.
I'll keep stabbing my heart for wanting
anything at all from you.

My friends tell me this won't end well.
Eventually, I'll want to be the gas from your gaslighting
and the flick of a lighter as you inhale.
I'll want to be the explosion,
the fire, the smoke,
and then gone.

The Edge

The darkness that fills the eyes of the escaped elephant,
moments before she is shot to death
on the streets of Honolulu,
comes to me in pieces—
sobs that I choke down
in the middle of a florescent day.

Our lives are unnatural transmigrations
from this uncertain world to the next,
and our souls are conglomerates of slaughtered, wild beauty.
I keep reaching out for the other,
but the other is wounded and blind.

One night I stopped time
and surveyed my life from a gold-speckled booth
at a 24-hour diner.
The lives around me simmered in smoke.
So much had happened that appeared
unlucky and random.
I realized that I was reaching the point
of more than I could handle
and wondered what might happen next.

New Orleans

Here, the ocean turned to stone, luck, and disaster.
Cemeteries crumble above ground and so do the ghosts,
dressed up in black, torn jackets and top hats.
Here, history not only repeats itself but sits down
and refuses to move. Musicians blossom
from the cracks in the sidewalk, mules stretch their necks
against the bit for an eternal summer,
and the Mississippi hums, lost in muddy reflections.

If you loiter in the Quarter for long, ghosts gather
about, assessing you as a possible host, hoping to relive
parts of their lives through you, but do not let them.
They will only cause chaos. I have seen pirates inhabiting
shop owners, their parrots prattling in several languages.
I have seen ghosts take over the body of drunks,
their faces morphing into the umber toned images
of Eugene Carriere. I have seen people dance,
and I have seen people fill up the streets with tears.

From Dauphine to Decatur, I followed
the lost, mournful notes of a valve trombone.
I trailed these notes through the streets
of the past and back to the present.

My heart stopped for a beat,
but it did not break
in the Vieux Carré.

Love and Clichés

Sometimes it seems like your life
is going to hell in a handbasket
while I'm living in a castle on a cloud
built by the wanderings of my imagination.

Somewhere between hell and sky,
we find time to see eye to eye
and to kiss as lovers do,
forgetting the world in the spark
and recognition of our skin.

We think a bit about death and taxes
which are far more certain than the apocalypse,
a word that rolls off tongues with ease these days.

Would you walk all day and night to save me
in a total grid shutdown, low flying fighter planes
making the earth a place few know how to navigate?

I love you more than I have loved any other,
but I don't have the same assurance
that I am the treasure you treasure.

I don't think a heart should be criticized
for feeling what it feels.
I don't think a mind should be condemned
for asking the questions it questions.
I don't want to feel alone at the end of the world.

Here's to a drop in the bucket,
and a dime in a wishing well.
Here's to feeling young again and believing
that love can conquer all, even our inner saboteurs.

Here's to turning my imaginary castle into one we own.
I know a few who make it look easy as child's play.

And Sometimes God

After the Wreck

How could I know that the world would have compassion
and that at the moment of impact my back would crack,

but I would retain the sensation of this body, first floating
away from it, then returning, silvered and open-mouthed

like a fish caught on the hook of a reoccurring dream,
struggling, flapping about, and jerked up to the surface

of a room full of florescence, tiny desires to survive
pulsing through my body in rivulets?

How could I know that the angels I recalled from paintings
would become bright, intelligent companions at the end of my bed

and that the torrential light from their eyes would answer my questions instantly?
How could I know that this peace would disintegrate like ice chips

in my mouth and this calming knowledge would drown in refills of morphine.
How could I know that I would never forget in the way that we forget dreams?

Dreamland

Give me guilt free days in an endless,
flooded dreamland of green,
wild alyssum and just born butterflies
a few feet away from our heavy heads, resting
on a quilt my grandmother made.
We might tell a few stories, and our kisses
might lead somewhere later than night,
or not, but our ties to earth and heaven
will be loosened, long enough to breathe
out molecules of our past and create
an enviable, simple,
present tense life.

Flying

Is the physical sensation of love.
Like a flock of startled Canadian geese
rising up from a pond.
Blood rising in your veins.
Fear. Anticipation.

If you have memories before birth
they are of flight,
of colors, of people
who you now know
and laughter.

The choice to experience
the eternal
in temporary
fleeting moments
is why we call love
falling.

Wise Sarasvati

Golden waves of light descend from the heavens
and fill my being. You need only listen to be healed.
As a kind soul, you must protect your kind nature.
Mention a small difficulty in your life
and observe the reactions of others. Connect with those
who draw near you with empathy.
Like butterflies, dart quickly from harm but do so lightly,
knowing your essential nature can never be injured
and resides in a realm beyond the physical.

Learn whose beaming smiles are insincere,
whose compliments manipulate,
whose presence will drain your energy
or add to your life force.

Prepare for what is destined to be. The notes of a symphony
will crescendo and fall in a universe made up of the love
inside of you. There is freedom in truth
and truth in a love that is free and vibrating
across the earth, free as the spirit you will become
and fly into a space I have opened for you now.

Milk and Honey:

Yitzak Rabin Speaks Minutes After His Assassination

"We should not let the land, flowing with milk and honey, become a land flowing with blood and tears. Don't let it happen," Rabin said.

I am struggling with being dead.

We spend our lives checking our watches,

riding upwards on an eternal escalator

and then suddenly, we are not visible

and given time to realize

our contribution to humanity.

What you read of my accomplishments

does not capture how I felt

or what and who I loved.

My immortal moment was no more

than the forcing of a little boy to shake hands with his enemy.

I became a magnet to my opposite—

Life to death, and then I merged with death.

We spend our lives planning ourselves

only to wad up the notes,

the grand outlines, and the photos in a fist.

We do not control all the factors

to color in our wishes as we want them.

Sometimes, they must sit above our heads

44

as clouds that change and blow away.
It is how it must be.
I have tapped out my dance,
and the dark curtain now hides my face.
You will know only what they tell you.

My role is no less,
no more
than another's role.
Listen to your drama teachers
because it takes all players to orchestrate
a moving production.

I look up, and I look down
as everything spins away from this blue world.
The joy here will render you
both heavy and light.

Walk slowly, my dears,
and appreciate everything.
I touch eternity now
the way a new born child reaches
toward the light
fresh with possibility.

Yitzhak Rabin (1 March 1922 – 4 November 1995) was an Israeli politician, statesman and general. He was the fifth Prime Minister of Israel, serving two terms in office, 1974−77 and 1992 until his assassination in 1995. In 1992, Rabin was re-elected as prime minister on a platform embracing the Israeli−Palestinian peace process. He signed several historic agreements with the Palestinian leadership as part of the Oslo Accords. In 1994, Rabin won the Nobel Peace Prize together with long-time political rival Shimon Peres and Palestinian leader Yasser Arafat. In November 1995, he was assassinated by an extremist named Yigal Amir, who opposed the terms of the Oslo Accords.

Be Like a Little Child

Before so many words
were scribbled across my memory,
I knew how to project myself
into a flock of birds.
I would close my eyes and fly
into the center of an orange sky.

When I rested my body on the grass,
melting into the earth like rain,
rabbits came so close
that I could hear them chew.

Faith was a concrete moment--
real as a conversation, a meal,
or a degree.
I was sunlight, and my heart
touched everything lightly.

Connected

I know that even when I am old, near-death,
possibly living in a house on a hill by myself,
my bones aching for release,
I will be connected to a sky full of angels
and a never-ending love from a compassionate God.

I'm only intimidating to those not yet as free,
those who have forgotten the wings of their spirits
those who have forgotten that we are here
for the music and gone quickly as a passing fantasy.

You tell me my life will be disappointing,
and I will be old, bitter, lonely, and then dead.
I would like to introduce you to my father—
a man who laughed and joked as death carried him away.
I'm that free too. I'm that certain.

Whatever this material world is—
it is only what we make of it.

Pain and hurt is destroyed in the fire that is my soul,
and I'll stay around to smile, sing an aria,
and exhale, a friend to all.

After the battle scars,
the slings and arrows of outrageous characters,
I can raise my glass of sparkling water and toast
to the happiness of everyone, for their happiness
is my happiness as well.

I'm more joyful than you can imagine.
Think sunlight, green pastures, hawks, and eagles.
Think evergreen trees, waterfalls, steep cliffs,
and hidden trails through a forest.
Think hiking by a stream and floating timeless in a lake.
Think laughter and esoteric study.

Think love, sweet lasting love.
Think better, not bitter, thoughts for me,
for you, and for all of us.

Energy

I'm a bullet train,
an over-caffeinated vein,
a marketer's wet dream,
a splurge, a spending spree,
a new degree, a carbohydrate high,
a late-night movie, a winning ticket,
hands thrown up to the heavens.

I'm a tiny ballerina in a jewelry box,
the one who knows just how to make you
want more.
I'm ruthless, careless, unlimited.
I'm free. I'm space. I'm candy. I'm the wild,
wild west of the world wide web.

I make billions in my sleep. Log off
into the deep waters of your unconscious
and you'll find me there. Faster
each nanosecond.
Conquering galaxies,
and conquering you.

New Show

Are you ever gonna change
or are you gonna keep floating
down imaginary rivers of pain in a land of plenty?
Will you create a home of darkness
in the middle of a neighborhood of love?

Will you blot out the sunshine with your rain clouds?
Will you run your vehicle into an embankment
instead of watching a matinee?
Will you blame those closest to you to avoid yourself,
and all the other roads that lead you peacefully home?

We all shuffle off this mortal coil,
and it is a relief,
not a punishment.
There's nothing to fear.
You leave your story on the ground.
You finally see how pride and victimization
are the same roles you fall for every time.

We are all in this together, not separately,
not in contradiction, not in competition.
You either elevate or deflate,
You either gravitate to the lighter side,
or stagnate in the void, in the absence of love.

Anopheline Mosquito to Malaria Victim

My life depends upon heat,
and I meant no harm.
The smell of your sweat and flesh mattered to me.
I have a constant hunger,
and you offered a reprieve from feelings
of frailty and transparency.

As you lie aching, sleepless,
clutching your stomach as you suffer,
please know that I cannot grasp
why my desire is also sickness.
In blindness, we hurt others.

Tonight, I will wait for emancipation.
The brightest streetlight
will swallow me whole,
erasing all fear.
On the other side, every transgression
is quickly forgiven.
There is only floating,
only love.

Last Email

There is no sorrow that eternity can't heal.
At this passage of tears and misunderstanding,
of flesh and only a certain amount of time remaining,
I tell you this bitterness is not true of me
and not true of you.
We are part flight of dove, part sunset, part rocky cliff
and streams. Don't forget the part of you
that dreams. It will matter more than you think.
I will see you there after this life, and all will be healed.

For the Love of Dogs

If I am lucky, one of my final gestures
in this life will be to reach out my right hand
and lay it gently on the canine companion at my side.

His ears will perk up as my spirit
shakes off this form.
My last gesture will be one of great love,
reaching out to the one
who was—even at his worst—adorable
and easy to forgive.

Meditation on Heaven

There would be music, of course,
and dancing. Maybe I have forgotten
how to delight in the golden hook
inside, the deep piercing, the point where flesh
is stuck but longs for Tuscany
and reflections on travel at the speed of light.

Parts of my consciousness flies ahead,
then returns blind,
whispering of a beauty
that contrasts with the present.

The closest I can come to perfection
is half-closed eyes, white wine
and bare feet, occasionally floating,
so light.

Flight

Don't dream about escape.
You are a rodent in the mouth
of a hawk. This happened too quickly.
Look at the sky for a while.

Admire how high all this has taken you.
Gaze into the sun for as long as you want.
Gaze until it blinds you.

Learning to love yourself fiercely
is what happens next.

A Prayer

Give me an eternity of green:
emerald bright and forest dark.

Grant me health:
a mind that extinguishes problems,
finds keys, makes comebacks,
never loses itself in dark, abysmal hovels
or mazes with walled in exits.

Offer me sympathetic sunlight
in the morning, warmth
that gives me energy
to breathe, to live.

Let God, the angels, and saints
send us all love to help us
float home
on a breeze of great peace.

His Favorite Painting

Paul Cézanne. House and Tree, L'Hermitage. c. 1874

The tree was both a protector and tormentor: an inventor of shadows
that danced through his mind and a maker of branches
that shielded him from the world like an angel mother
reaching out her arms to rock him to sleep.

He returned home only late at night,
off center from a night of trivia at the bar—
anything to distract him from the relentless, confusing dreams,
unusual emotions, and headaches that brought him to his knees.

The words could not come fast enough to fill in the empty places
in the sky, the stretch of country, the lack of contact,
the blur of vision, and the beginning of winter.

He called his neighbor, his daughter,
and an ambulance when it became obvious
that the battle to hang on to his house
and his tree had been lost.

Everything Works Out for the Best

Your death feels like you have gone fishing
and never returned to the job that filled your clothes
with sweat, the wife who slung curses at you,
wanting more love from you than she knew how to say.

Each night, I picture you resting beneath a blinking motel sign
that reads *vacancy*, and your dreams are thick
with pine trees, spatters of stars, and animal eyes.

Against all odds, you believed that everything
has way of working out for the best,
that poverty doesn't matter when you can tell a good story,
and all that we love comes back to us.

Nothing worked out according to plan (if there ever was one)
or even favorably in your life,
but even a grapefruit-sized brain tumor couldn't kill your humor.
Death only made you shrug, unbelieving.

Wild man, father, I set your ashes free
in the lake of your waking dreams,
wondering if other fishermen could feel the luxury of the sun,
the deep mud, the silvery fins, and the rush of motors skimming
the surface of the water as their eventual heaven.

Too Eager

In anticipation of flowers
I take the hummingbird's beat
as my own

...much too fast for the long termination
of the human life span

...all flutter and wild, dilated eyes
black holes burning
for a flash of red
or streak of yellow pollen

...miscalculation of real
reflected in glass

and I crash.

Grit

The night sky opened up into a bright noon,
and I joined a circle of boat lovers
with glittering eyes and weathered skin.
We donned white hats and looked at art,
looked at poems, always searching for salvation
in the sky, the salt, and the air of spring.
I didn't know then that once I became a pilgrim,
I would always be a pilgrim in need
of gulls and sunsets.

***

Oh Lord, I have slammed doors shut
with superhuman strength,
with centuries of hate and vengeance,
but you keep whispering of a way out
and through these words I find it.

***

Not the waves, not the laughter,
not the sticky chairs and unopened wine,
but the feeling near the end.
Light began to seep into everything we touched.
We may have been born into darkness,

but we eventually learned how to sail
through any weather.

Spring Evening

One star, one bird, one sky
filled with billions of dreams,
and something tender connecting each of us
to our childhoods—
the first time we wondered
how far the sky extended and spent slow moments
thinking about eternity and what it might mean
to never die, to simply keep flying to the next galaxy
and the next, far away from all the stories
we had not yet created.

We came into this world
with the Milky Way in the light in our eyes
and magic in our tiny fingertips. All of time was no time.

Beauty multiplied wherever
our gazes landed, and if I had one wish tonight
it would be that everyone could feel harmony—
no empty spaces, no ragged edges,
no knife wounds cutting
through the soul.

Whole.

Coming Up Aces

I wouldn't believe it if it hadn't have happened
the way it happened. Four aces in my hand.
Only a couple of lucky days in my entire chaotic life,
and now everything is moving like an arrow set aflame.
Instant vibrational love match, success at work,
meaningful hobbies, supportive friends,
good health, recognition, numerous awards,
and wonderful dinners that I don't have to cook.
Miraculously, my life is almost as fantastic
as my social media profile makes it appear.

Express Life

Time races near the end, but how much
velocity can we endure, shifting our aching bodies
from one position to another.

Do we eventually adjust to the flash of the high-speed choices,
protein-packed snacks, and all that is difficult to process?

How many galaxies will we locate, and will this help us
know God, or will we, somewhere between the enormity
and the miniscule, simply close our eyes, smile, and ride.

Healed

I no longer resonate with poetry that tears open
the self into thousands of painful images.
I'll take the dark sunglasses though, and read *New Yorker* cartoons,
drink hot tea with almond milk, and meditate.

I got older and my balance improved.
I can stand in tree pose for hours.
I recovered some childhood joy, retrograded all the way
back to the spark of God and held on to that spark
like a winning 90-million-dollar lottery ticket.

I'm not knocking the need to share the gruesome details
of a dark night of the soul. It beats repression,
and I've been there, have a few trophies
from the weeks where I shuffled down hallways
like a lost princess in sweats swallowing a rationed pill
that made me sleep like I was resting on a cloud.

Expression and anger can get you off the couch
and into the world which is the first step.
So, go ahead, my dears, scream into your microphones.
Wipe off your sweaty palms and receive your earned applause.
All I'm saying is that if you chase healing long enough,
you can find it within yourself. Remember that.

All This Talk About Death

We go on folks...we go *on*.
The credits are rolling,
surgeons are packing up their tools,
loved ones are falling to their knees,
and there you are in spirit going on,
finally aware of how your worries
shouldn't have been worries.

You should have loved them more,
hugged them more frequently,
reminded them to be happier,
taken them out to enjoy the sunlight and moonlight.

You should have danced more,
laughed more, praised more,
and joked around a bit more.

You are excited though,
hovering there above your discarded body
because it makes more sense to continue
than to become nothing when you are something—
a spark of God that you dimmed
and brightened depending on your circumstances and mood.

And, now, you can be fully who you were meant to be,
who you too often limited in the realm of fear and time.

ABOUT THE AUTHOR

Tricia Barker experienced a profound near-death experience during her senior year of college, and this experience guided her to teach overseas, in public schools, and at the college level. Her near-death experience story has been featured on *I Survived: Beyond and Back*, *National Geographic Magazine, Simple Grace Magazine, Women's World Magazine*, and *The Doctor Oz Show*.

Tricia's memoir, *Angels in the OR: What Dying Taught Me About Healing, Survival, and Transformation* is also available through Audible. This book tells a story of her near-death experience, teaching mission, and eventual triumph over trauma in her past.

Tricia is a graduate of The University of Texas. She also received her MFA in Creative Writing from Goddard College. Currently, she teaches English and Creative Writing at a beautiful community college in Fort Worth, Texas. She interviews other near-death experiencers, researchers, healers, spiritual teachers, and authors on her YouTube Channel. Tricia's poetry and essays have been published in several publications including *The Binnacle, The Paterson Literary Review*, and *The Midwest Quarterly*.

Website www.triciabarkernde.com

www.ingramcontent.com/pod-product-compliance
Lightning Source LLC
Chambersburg PA
CBHW080522090426
42734CB00015B/3135